LEARN TO TELL THE TIME

with the

MUNCH BUNCH

Library of Congress in Publication Data

Reed, Giles.
  Learn to tell time with the Munch Bunch.

  Summary: Provides for practice in telling time as
the Munch Bunch prepares for a picnic at the beach.
  1. Clocks and watches—Juvenile literature. 2. Time—
Juvenile literature. [1. Time] I. Mitson, Angela, ill.
II. Title.
TS548.R4 1981   529'.7   81-12042
ISBN 0-86625-080-8   AACR2

Rourke Publications, Inc.
Windermere, FL   32786

THIS IS A CLOCK

It has one big hand for the minutes,
and one little hand for the hours

MINUTE   There are 60 seconds in one minute
HOUR   There are 60 minutes in one hour
DAY   There are 24 hours in one day

Twelve o'clock One o'clock Two o'clock Three o'clock Four o'clock Five o'clock

Six o'clock   Seven o'clock   Eight o'clock   Nine o'clock   Ten o'clock   Eleven o'clock

A DAY IN THE LIFE OF THE MUNCH BUNCH

The first hour of their day

It is eight o'clock

The Munch Bunch are getting up ~

ready for the day ahead

It is five minutes past eight
The Munch Bunch decide to go to the seaside

It is ten minutes past eight

Spud prepares the Munch Bunch car

It is a quarter past eight
Lizzie Leek and her friends prepare the sandwiches

 It is twenty minutes past eight

Suzie and Penny are filling the basket

 It is twenty-five minutes past eight

Casper Carrot looks worried - as usual

It is half past eight
Tom and Bounce are mending the deck chairs

It is twenty~five minutes to nine

Olly has found his fishing~rod

It is twenty minutes to nine

Supercool is looking for his swimming trunks

It is a quarter to nine
**Billy and Scruff are being naughty
~as usual**

It is ten minutes to nine
Zach Zucchini has collected the sports equipment

It is five minutes to nine

Everyone is getting very excited

 It is nine o'clock

The Munch Bunch leave for the seaside

MORNING
It is eleven o'clock in the morning
Everyone is having a nice time

AFTERNOON
It is three o'clock in the afternoon
It is time to have a picnic

EVENING
It is seven o'clock in the evening
It is time to go home

NIGHT

It is ten o' clock at night

And everyone is tucked in fast asleep

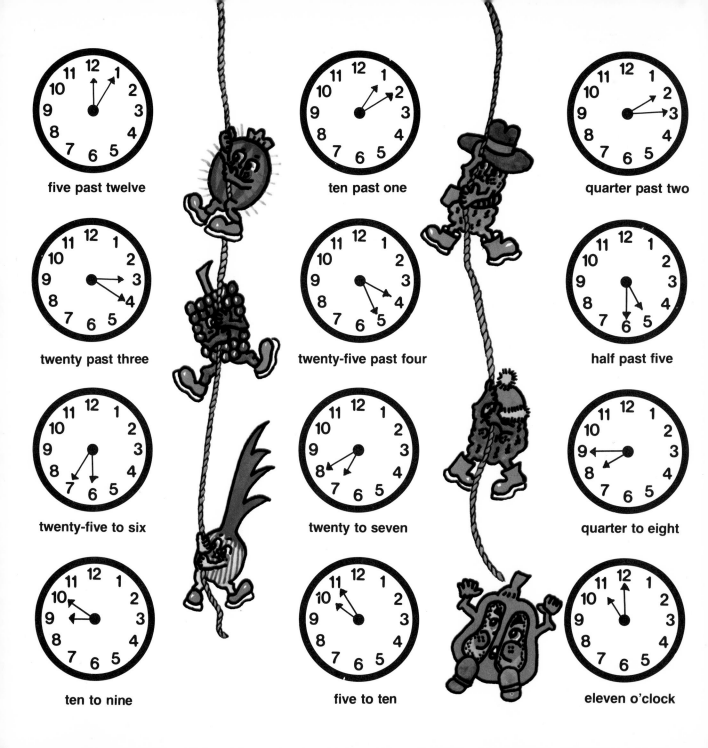

five past twelve

ten past one

quarter past two

twenty past three

twenty-five past four

half past five

twenty-five to six

twenty to seven

quarter to eight

ten to nine

five to ten

eleven o'clock